My Mother Never Died Before

&

Other Poems

Marcia B. Loughran

Second Place Winner of The Poetry Box Chapbook Prize 2020

Editing, Book & Cover Design: Shawn Aveningo Sanders
Cover Ilustration: Josephine Sanders
Author photo: Cam Sanders Photography

ISBN: 978-1-948461-72-6
Printed in the United States of America.
Wholesale Distribution via Ingram.

Published by The Poetry Box®, 2021
Portland, Oregon
ThePoetryBox.com

With thanks to all the members of this club
who shared their "How I lost my mother" stories,
especially Sam, Jim and Brian

Yes, I know who you are, said the baby bird.
You are not a kitten. You are not a hen.
You are not a dog. You are not a cow.
You are not a boat....
You are a bird, and you are my mother.

—*Are You My Mother?* P.D. Eastman,
Random House Children's Books, 1960

You're not the only pebble on the beach.

—Betsy Sanders, 1935-2019

Contents

after

Nobody Knew What It Was

Imagining a *columbarium* to be
a place of honor and glory,
wisteria and tapering vines

my aunt and uncle wandered around the grounds
for half an hour,
finally peering into a little window

in the door of a small shed,
startling the security guard
sleeping inside—

Is this the columbarium?
My uncle asked a little hopelessly.
The what-now? The guard replied.

Turns out it is a wall
at the back door
of the church

we walked by every day
on the way to school
never noticing the flowers

or their changing.
Inside: small vaults
under slabs of rock

that lift up
like trap doors
to reveal a little cupboard,

[. . .]

I imagined—I don't know—I looked away
when the priest deposited
the box of ashes.

You have to stand right over it
looking down
to see the quiet names.

Bird's eye view.

Awareness of Birds

After my mother died
everything became about the birds—
I was comforted by sparrows,
chunky, dun-colored,
hard to differentiate from winter itself,
clustered among threadbare branches.
Birds signified
presence, persistence, peace, maybe.
A female cardinal
hopping around a sycamore
fussing over a dead leaf
felt like a message.
Feathers on the sidewalk
pointed the right direction.
Even pigeons
dive-bombing trash
in the intersection
as we waited for the light to turn—
backlit and holy.
A single swan
among the geese
at the edge of the East River
so clearly my long-necked mother—
Just checking in!
Making sure
we were all right.

My Mother Never Died Before

It's been three weeks
since my mother died and I am starting
to forget, not her, to forget
each crazy mini-moment since,
how the EMT got on the phone with me—
it's what we all want,
our own bed, our own pajamas—
how the next day
Kevin from the funeral home
pronounced *pah-JAY-mas*
the way they do in the Midwest,
she'll be dressed
in a new set of pah-JAY-mas—
he is from Ohio,
although a different part
than my mother.
Just being from Ohio
felt like a miracle to us
as we stood in the parlor of Grommer's Sons,
which incidentally *did*
Presidents Taft, Roosevelt, Roosevelt, JFK—
then I stopped listening
because we walked into a room full of coffins—
thoughtfully laid out like new cars,
angled to imagine an exciting journey in comfort and safety—
some open to white quilted interiors,
some closed to accentuate a glossy finish.
I kept saying, *Uh! Ugh! Uck!!* as we passed through
which was probably rude.
But Kevin never blinked—
he is a professional—
and when my brother and I

squabbled, you could tell
Kevin had a sister somewhere—
maybe in Ohio—
he would squabble with, too.
Walking towards the urn display
my father spied a tasteful wooden box
holding tissues—
She'd love that one! he said.
Even Kevin laughed.
It made looking at the urns easy, I was surprised
how simple, I'd imagined a Grecian vase
with curvatures and animals in blue
cavorting, not these plain wooden containers
bigger than a toaster
smaller than a breadbox.
We picked one and wandered out
making small talk about the renovations.
I want to remember
the scraps of things,
what people say, offerings,
a patchwork quilt to comfort us—
moments of incredulity, this is
happening,
my mother has died, the event
I have been dreading and preparing for,
imagining the possibility,
possibly since I was born.
Here is how it felt to get the news:
like the boat I had been sailing
thudded into a dock.
Like I stepped onto the pier and held
the stillness of land

[. . .]

after a long time afloat—
my sea-legs stopped rocking.
Maybe because the cord
that had been gently, persistently
tugging me along,
pulling me over the ocean,
the cord
that yanked me into the world
has been cut.

Cleaning Out My Mother's Purse on Mother's Day

I didn't mean to
I thought sitting on a chair
in my father's study
while he sat at his desk
would help him
shuffle through medieval towers of paper,
stuffed manila envelopes, decades of tax receipts, bills,
a legacy of piles.
My sister had tried
to organize,
evidence of her fits and starts
the occasional labeled folder,
shiny new boxes, empty,
no match for the file cabinet,
top drawer jammed off its rails,
the color of illness and being stuck indoors.
To look busy I picked up the cardboard box
blocking the closet door
and happened to find
my mother's purse
someone had thrown there
in the panic of death and moving.
Ugly and utilitarian,
black nylon material,
sensible shoulder strap
to hang on the kitchen chair
so she could reach it
to get the checkbook before church—
Hand me my purse—

[. . .]

Inside: inhaler, tissues, a plastic comb,
some ancient inedible mints
I pocketed
like magic pebbles from a stream.

Inheritance

I have my mother's voice.
Train rolling by on an overheard track voice.
Gravel coming down from a hole in the ceiling voice.
Alto with a rusty edge.

I have my mother's voice.
The voice I never hated
when I hated her,
when I was a teenager and hated everything.

She didn't have her mother's voice, or her father's,
it came out of nowhere
low and loud,
not a lot of ladylike.

After she died
I erased her voicemails—
I have her voice
inside my head.

I have my mother's voice
from when she was my age.
As she ran out of air it got hoarse, croaky,
thickly clogged like her lungs.

She had no pain.
She liked to point out
the ladies in church
worse off than her—

[. . .]

Poor Nan, she'd say, *Look at Nellie—*
can you imagine a back brace?
This from a blind woman in a wheelchair
with two tanks of oxygen on the back.

She loved a tower of seafood,
licking her lips
at the lobster and clams.
She lived on white wine.

I don't miss her
much.
I have my mother's
voice.

Phone Calls

There's a specific time of day—
not a time exactly,
more like a pause

after the second cup of coffee,
before I get dressed and go to work—
I could be paying the phone bill or folding the laundry—

I feel like calling my mother.
Nothing urgent, more
like I have nothing

to say and she was always
the best at listening to nothing,
all the nothings that happen in a day.

As it happens, today I have a story
she would've liked to hear
about my friend

who was biking home
up Madison Avenue, crossed 41st Street
and woke up

surrounded by EMT's.
No idea what happened,
no memory of the people who helped.

He lay on a stretcher in the ER for hours—
immobilized in a neck brace—
listening to the man on the left,

[. . .]

withdrawing from heroin,
and the man on the right,
who had mixed up his meds,

both of them frequent flyers,
neither of them visible
to my friend, who couldn't move his head.

Other than 12 staples in his skull
and an overwhelming desire to nap,
he's ok.

What I wanted to tell my mother
was how I laughed out loud
at the image of my friend

in a neck brace, because neck braces
are funny. Just to see
what she would say,

am I a bad person
to laugh at this story,
laugh out loud in relief?

I think she'd be just as relieved,
she likes this friend. And so pleased
at further evidence of miracles.

The fact that I'm not sad
I can't tell this story to my mother:
another, more minor miracle.

It's hard to laugh
and be sad
at the same time,

like trying to keep your eyes open
when you sneeze.
Not sad for that brief moment.

And how can anyone be sad
when my friend
didn't die there at 41st and Madison

didn't ruin everyone's Thanksgiving,
and can call me up
and tell me all about it?

Differences of Opinion

If there is a heaven,
which my mother said there wasn't,
she is there, arguing
with her mother
about the color of the kitchen.

If there is a heaven,
you get to decorate it
the way you want
and in our family, kitchens are yellow.
But yellow is a wide road.

Betsy! Too bright!
says my grandmother—
It's not a New York taxi.
Gran's already joined the country club,
started a local chapter of Colonial Dames,

put my mother's name on every list—
You'll get in, she says. For Gran,
kitchens are for sit-down breakfast,
matching saucers, eggcups,
milk in a bone china jug.

Her yellow a watery winter sunlight,
squinty with a memory of warmth.
My mother? Butter and popcorn,
a three-year-old's drawing of the sun.
Dandelions, daffodils.

Odd they are fighting
about color; they both
had macular degeneration
the last ten years of their lives.
Faces, edges gone. Only color remained.

Color kept them going,
they had color in common.
Because it is heaven and harmony required,
they take turns
clambering up the ladder

in angelic white overalls
splattered with a rainbow of *corn, sunflower,*
lemon, butterscotch, bumblebee,
chamomile and *Chardonnay*—
painting and repainting each other's walls.

before

Christmas Memory

The meanest thing I ever did
to my mother
over a long career of catty remarks,
killer stares, ice-storms and obnoxious
adolescent behaviors
everything everything was her fault

the very meanest, if it is possible
to measure mean on a scale
of snippy to murderous,
of course
everything everything
was her fault, not mine

not my fault we moved to Connecticut
senior year of high school
not my fault I didn't have a friend
in that white clapboard town
of green clapboard shutters,
I've never known such tall hedges.

I took long, solitary walks to the river
and wished it was the sea. The meanest thing
I ever did was to laugh
at the home-made ornaments
my mother had crafted from pinecones and seashells
collected on her long, solitary walks.

Glittered and glued
with ribbons and felt
to decorate the Christmas tree.
We hadn't brought our Christmas boxes,

[. . .]

we were only staying a year—
all her fault.

Because my heart was full of poison,
I taunted her for each and every tiny pinecone
with its twisted wire hook.
My sister and brothers joined in—
a menacing choir of mockery—
until my mother left the room in tears.

Her fault we sat in silence,
her monsters.
No one went after her.
She says she doesn't remember
when I ask about it now,
the time I was the meanest.

For thirty-three years, wherever I live,
a padded manila envelope arrives
in December. Inside:
a small, single branch of evergreen
tied with red ribbon,
no card.

By the Window in the Winter

Branches blank as train tracks.
We listen for the whistle of spring
coming around the corner,
crossing the river.
The neighbor's tree
(always the first)
has tiny buds
which weren't there
yesterday, I swear.

The neighbor
who we thought died last week.
Her funeral, if it was hers,
did not include us,
though the houseful on the left
departed dressed for grief
in bright display
some in a somber limo,
some walking, coatless.

If not for her, then
who had died and not
invited us? No matter,
red buds are here;
she may be or
she may not. I am
trying to accept
my life for what it is.

My mother called me, twice,
to let me know
the gardenia bloomed.

She lives four hours south;
she likes being the harbinger of spring.
We all lose something
as we age. In my family
we forget or we go blind.
She went blind. Or
she can't see everything—
faces, pages of a book.
Color she kept—
white gardenia blossoms
amidst the dishes and the mail
on the kitchen table.

Burdened Vessel

That vessel which, according to the applicable Navigation Rules, must give way to the privileged vessel. The term has been superseded by the term 'give-way.'
—Nautical Know-How Glossary of Nautical Terms

We live in a buoy
without a bell,
portable for river trips,
night festivals.

My mother's circulation
maps the riverbed:
sunspot mudflats
ancient arteries.

She packs teacups,
I think I hear a whistle at the door.

We live in a house
made of keyholes—
wind peeks in
air leaks out

I tape up gaps.
Every month the doctor puts a needle
in my mother's eyes
to help her see.

She squints
and abdicates the periscope.

[. . .]

We live in a birch bark canoe—
it is tippy.
I decree, *No more falls,*
but a fall in this house has no reason.

Remove all wires!
Clear the rocks!
She staggers,
held up by three windows.

We nap to the sound of rapids
which will waterfall downriver.

We live in a claw-foot bathtub,
her soggy cough
a foghorn we ignore
like the radio. Same cough

rocked me to sleep
before I was born.
I circle the tub with tubing,
reset the compass.

We sit at our portholes,
watch the light shift slowly

from the one on the left in the morning
to the one on the right at night—

she paddles light,
I bail with a thimble.

Our shrinking ballast:
air   water   time.

Baghdad, 1963

Teahouses lined the dusty streets of the old river town.
On weekends, my parents left my sister, their first baby, home

asleep in the lap of Hannifa, the Kurdish cook, and drove into the dunes
to camp. They woke before dawn to walk the coolest hours of the day

among scattered bricks of ancient Sumerian villages,
looking for artifacts on the surface of the sand:

broken bits of pottery, figurines, beads, all that was left
of neatly irrigated fields and mud-brick villages

destroyed by Mongols from the North. As the sun rose
over Zagros Mountain, my parents prowled near Eridu,

entrance to the underworld. When Sumerians descended
to the watery kingdom, they did not go unarmed.

The dead were buried with maces, wooden staffs,
provisions for their journey. What will my parents bring

on their last walk? May they amble together,
two tall Americans, hats on, heads down. A willowy blonde

with legs up to here and the man she followed into the desert.
My father sings a ditty he wrote for cabaret night at the club,

my mother sighs and smokes a cigarette. They pocket amulets,
bicker over origins, gossip about the ones they leave behind.

Tap Dance at the Nursing Home

I want to write a poem for my brother,
for packing his tap shoes, portable speaker,

big straw hat—
for flying to Wyoming for my birthday

promising to dance.
His talent show's next week in California.

When the time came,
he didn't want to, he wasn't ready,

so perhaps this is a poem for my mother,
who sent an urgent message:

Don't forget to do your dance.
So he did, he danced for us

dudes, ranch hands, cabin girls,
then flew to Massachusetts to dance

for my mother,
who couldn't get to Wyoming.

He doesn't have the routine down,
there are gaps

serious, sweaty giraffe of a man,
tapping his way across America.

Why tap? I asked when he started classes.
He said, *Fifty and cancer.*

I want to write a poem for my brother getting better:
that poem has to wait.

On his way to Logan Airport after dancing for my mother,
my brother stopped by Sunrise Manor Nursing

to see his friend George from high school.
George is there because of his brain

and he's not going home.
When my brother arrived, the room was empty.

They were all in the lounge at the sing-along,
George the youngest by thirty-five years.

Maybe this is a poem for George.
When the singing was over

and the tambourines still,
my brother offered to dance

for George and a roomful of strangers—
old folks, nurses, singers.

I forgot the middle of the second number—
it doesn't matter, it's all practice,

he told me, boarding the flight home.
Is this a poem for the people in wheelchairs,

people we will become,
people some of us are?

[. . .]

Or is it for me
and for you?

Diminished, not dead,
bemused by the dance

we invent as we go.
Why poems? You ask.

I say, *Forty and infertility.*
Let this be our poem:

Don't forget to do your dance.
My brother's tap show is Monday

at the Electric Lodge in Venice—
everybody's welcome.

Acknowledgments

Poems in this manuscript have appeared, some in slightly different form, in the following publications:

"By the Window in the Winter" in *Still Life with Weather,* 2016.

"Burdened Vessels" in *The Santa Clara Review,* Volume 104, Issue 1, February 2017.

"Baghdad, 1963" in *Ellipsis Literature and Art,* Volume 53, 2017.

"Tap Dance at the Nursing Home" in *Verdad Magazine, Literature and Art,* Volume 26, Spring 2019.

"My Mother Never Died Before" in *Still Against War: Poems for Marie Ponsot,* Vol. IX, 2019.

"Phone Calls" in *Still Against War: Poems for Marie Ponsot,* Vol. X, 2020.

Thank You

Cam and Jim, my first readers. Nick for five-dollar words and faithful copy-editing. Jojo for the beautiful cover. Nancy and Franny, my pandemic writing group. Jackson, Katherine, Jamie, Nan and Howard, the Poetry Gang. David, Corinne, Tracey, Seana, Isabella, Wendy, and Olive for always wanting to hear another. Sarah Fearon and the Irish American Writers and Artists for resounding cheers. My father, who taught me to write. My mother, who taught me to read. And David Loughran, who feeds me, waters me and continues to surprise me almost every day.

Praise for My Mother Never Died Before

My Mother Never Died Before is a joyful read, full of surprises. Marcia B. Loughran shows her versatility and variety while bringing a welcome dose of humor to this collection, which is hard to pull off in poems about death. The many familiar scenes here—shopping for caskets, cleaning out papers after a parent has died, touching their intimate objects like breath mints and combs—are all painted with such clarity and reality. Loughran takes a risk by beginning with the "after" poems and ending with the "before," but the gamble pays off beautifully—the innocence of "before" makes the "after" all the more poignant in retrospect.

—Amy Miller, Contest Judge, 2020
and author of *The Trouble with New England Girls*

In our family, kitchens are yellow./ But yellow is a wide road, Marcia B. Loughran writes in "Differences of Opinion," one of a dozen in her exquisitely-rendered palette of poems *My Mother Never Died Before.* Loughran is a master colorist, depicting the sort of home I always wanted to grow up in or, at least, have next door: The one with that yellow-walled kitchen (the exact shade being *Button and popcorn/ a three-year-old's drawing of the sun./ Dandelions, daffodils*), *a patchwork quilt to comfort us/ moments of incredulity,* and most of all, full of good company with whom to spend time—one of this book's primary pleasures.

Another is its understated wit: *It's hard to laugh/ and be sad/ at the same time,/ like trying to keep your eyes open/ when you sneeze,* Loughran writes in "Phone Calls" a poem that in part deliberates, with a certain gallows humor, on the comical nature of neck braces. "Burdened Vessel," on the other hand, exerts a breathtaking gravitas, using nautical imagery as a metaphor for the sacrifices of caretaking, a stunning achievement of magical realism which resonates as deeply as *her soggy cough/ a foghorn we ignore/ like the radio.*

Throughout, with the strength of language precise yet lyrical, odd but familiar, full of heart though refreshingly void of even a hint of the saccharine, Loughran has written a eulogy that would make any mother proud, even (or perhaps especially) when she allows, in "Inheritance," that *I don't miss her/ much.*

—Lissa Kiernan, author of *Two Faint Lines in the Violet*
and Founding Director of the Poetry Barn

In these twelve terse, keenly observed, and often heartbreaking poems, Marcia B. Loughran excavates and articulates the liminal space of grief, telescoping in and around the strangest of moments—when you lose the person who gave you life. Loughran expertly captures the puzzlement and unmoored nature of losing one's mother. And in each poem, she gives us tantalizing clues about who was lost and who was left behind. The mother at the center of these poems emerges as someone who was witty, adventurous and, above all, kind. I found myself longing to sit in her yellow kitchen while making home-made Christmas ornaments over a cup of tea, with milk from a *bone china jug*. The love between the mother and daughter in this volume is not flashy, it feels quiet but deeply rooted and the grief the daughter experiences is a subtle ache, encapsulated by Loughran's perfect lines, *I feel like calling my mother./ Nothing urgent, more/ like I have nothing/ to say and she was always/ the best at listening to nothing/ all the nothings that happen in a day.*

—Cusi Cram, playwright, screenwriter
and Arts Professor at Tisch School of the Arts

Marcia B. Loughran's vulnerable, heartfelt poems brought me comfort I did not know I needed. Her clear, honest imagery portrayed simple snapshots of daily life that brought my Grandma back to me. Anyone who has felt alone and lost after the death of a loved one will be comforted by Loughran's honest telling of her own grieving. Through her profound poems, Loughran bravely explores the pain of death contrasted with the power of memories.

—Lillian Sanders, author
Navigating the Afterlife and Other Reasons to Cut Class

About the Author

Marcia B. Loughran won Mrs. Mott's prestigious haiku prize in fifth grade at the National Cathedral School in Washington, D.C., and resumed her writing career thirty years later. She received an MFA in Creative Writing from the Bennington Writing Seminars in 2013.

Her work has appeared in *The New York Times, Verdad, Spoon River Poetry Review* and elsewhere. Marcia's first chapbook, *Still Life with Weather,* won the 2016 WaterSedge Poetry Chapbook Prize. She reads her work in various bars, bookstores and black-box theaters in New York City and the Catskills and is a regular at the Irish American Writers and Artists' Salons. Marcia is a nurse practitioner and lives in Queens, NY.

<https://marciabloughran.com>

The Poetry Box Chapbook Prize

In 2018, The Poetry Box® introduced their annual Chapbook Prize competition. The contest is open to both established poets and emerging talent alike, and the editors reserve the right to select more than one poet's manuscript for publication. Currently, the contest is open to poets residing in the United States and is open for submissions each year during the month of February. Find more information at ThePoetryBox.com.

2020 Winners:

The Day of My First Driving Lesson by Tiel Aisha Ansari

My Mother Never Died Before by Marcia B. Loughran

Off Coldwater Canyon by C.W. Emerson

2019 Winners:

Moroccan Holiday by Lauren Tivey

Hello, Darling by Christine Higgins

Falling into the River by Debbie Hall

2018 Winners:

Shrinking Bones by Judy K. Mosher

November Quilt by Penelope Scambly Schott

14: Antología del Sonoran by Christopher Bogart

Fireweed by Gudrun Bortman

CPSIA information can be obtained
at www.ICGtesting.com
Printed in the USA
BVHW090525021220
594419BV00008BA/153

9 781948 461726